The Northern Lights

Susan Canizares

SCHOLASTIC INC.

NEW YORK • TORONTO • LONDON • AUCKLAND • SYDNEY

Acknowledgments

Science Consultants: Patrick R. Thomas, Ph.D., Bronx Zoo/Wildlife Conservation Park;
Glenn Phillips, The New York Botanical Garden; **Literacy Specialist:** Maria Utefsky,
Reading Recovery Coordinator, District 2, New York City

Design: MKR Design, Inc.

Photo Research: Barbara Scott

Endnotes: Susan Russell

Photographs: Cover: Michio Hoshino/Minden Pictures; p. 1: Gordon Garradd/Science Photo
Library/Photo Researchers, Inc.; p. 2: Michio Hoshino/Minden Pictures; p. 3: Jack Finch/Science
Photo Library/Photo Researchers, Inc.; p. 4: B & C Alexander/Photo Researchers, Inc.; pp. 5 & 6-7:
S. Nielsen/DRK Photo; pp. 8-9: Pekka Parviainen/Science Photo Library/Photo Researchers; pp. 10-
11 & 12: S. Neilsen/DRK Photo;

Library of Congress Cataloging-in-Publication Data
Canizares, Susan, 1960-
The northern lights / Susan Canizares.
p. cm. -- (Science emergent readers)
"Scholastic early childhood."
Includes index.
Summary: Focuses on the beauty of the colors found in the northern lights.
ISBN 0-590-76155-2 (pbk.: alk. paper)
1. Auroras--Juvenile literature. 2 [1. Auroras. 2. Color.]
I. Title. II. Series.
QC971.4.C23 1998

538'.768--dc21

97-34210
CIP AC

30 29 28 27 26 25 24 23 22 21   03

red

yellow

blue

green

purple

purple and blue

red and yellow

purple and green

What colors do you see?

Northern Lights

On clear nights, far in the north, the skies can be filled with great sheets of shimmering light. The light patterns dance and move and come in many different colors. This amazing display is called the "aurora borealis," or northern lights.

Who gets to see the northern lights? The people who live near the polar regions in countries such as Finland, Alaska, Canada, and Russia can see them. Sometimes, people who live as far south as Maine get treated to this great light show. The colors of the northern lights are most often frosty white or pale blues and greens, but the lights have been seen in every color of the rainbow.

What creates the northern lights? Well, the earth is like a huge magnet, and the earth's north and south poles are like the ends of the magnet. The poles attract particles in the atmosphere that are tiny bits of energy. Some of these bits of energy come from the sun and they are called solar particles. Sometimes, the sun puts out extra amounts of energy and creates what we call solar flares. This greater amount of solar energy gives rise to the northern lights.

These extra solar particles flow around and around the earth, but in outer space. As they flow, they sometimes come near the north and south poles of the earth. And because the poles are the ends of the earth's magnet, they capture some of the solar particles, bringing them into the earth's atmosphere. Now the particles collide with gaseous particles already in the atmosphere. When they collide like this, they give off light and that light is what we see in the sky. This spectacular effect is called the aurora. Shown in this book is the "aurora borealis" in the far north. In the far south, this light show is called the "aurora australis."